Neil Morris

ISLAM

Grange
BOOKS

TABLE OF CONTENTS

Note – This book shows dates as related to the conventional beginning of our era, or the year 0, understood as the year of Christ's birth. All events dating before this year are listed as BCE, or Before Current Era (ex. 928 BCE). Events dating after the year 0 are defined as CE, or Current Era (ex. 24 CE), wherever confusion might arise.

WORLD OF BELIEFS

In the same series:
- Judaism
- Christianity
- Buddhism

Published by Grange Books
an imprint of Grange Books Plc
The Grange
Kingsnorth Industrial Estate
Hoo, nr Rochester
Kent ME3 9ND
www.Grangebooks.co.uk

ISBN 1-84013-598-0
Grange Books edition printed in 2004

Islam
was created and produced by McRae Books
Borgo Santa Croce, 8 – Florence (Italy)
info@mcraebooks.com

SERIES EDITOR Anne McRae
TEXT Neil Morris
ILLUSTRATIONS Studio Stalio (Alessandro Cantucci, Fabiano Fabbrucci,
Andrea Morandi), Paola Ravaglia, Gian Paolo Faleschini, Daniela Astone
GRAPHIC DESIGN Marco Nardi
LAYOUT Laura Ottina, Adriano Nardi
REPRO Litocolor, Florence
PICTURE RESEARCH Elzbieta Gontarska
Printed and bound in China

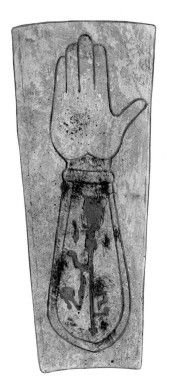

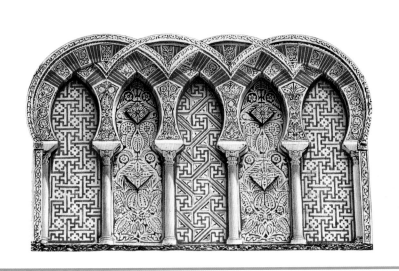

Introduction

The **Islamic** religion began almost 1,400 years ago in what is now Saudi Arabia, when the Prophet **Muhammad** received revelations from God. The revelations were written down in a holy book called the **Qur'an**, and Muhammad's followers and successors soon spread the word of Islam beyond Arabia. To Muslims – the followers of Islam – their religion became a way of life, forming and guiding their entire culture and society. Islam's teachings have spread around the world and the Muslim population numbers more than a billion people.

The crescent moon and star form the symbol of Islam, which appears on many national flags.

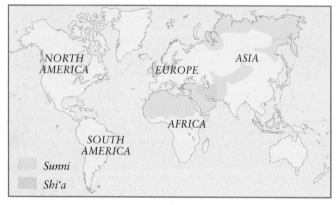

Regions of the world where the two main branches of Islam are dominant.

A world religion

Muslims make up almost a fifth of the world's population today. The main regions where Islam is dominant include the Middle East, southwest, central, and Southeast Asia, and North Africa. On other continents, including North America and Europe, there are sizable minority Muslim communities. Well over three-quarters of the world's Muslims follow the **Sunni** branch of Islam.

A Sunni scholar at the court of the Ottoman emperor in the 16th century.

Shi'ites

The majority of people in Iran and Iraq follow the Shi'a branch of Islam. Its name comes from the Arabic Shi'at Ali, meaning "party of Ali." **Shi'ites** do not accept the first three Sunni **caliphs** and regard Ali, the fourth caliph, as Muhammad's first true successor. They believe that the leader of Islam must be a descendant of Ali, Muhammad's cousin and son-in-law.

This Shi'ite standard bears the names of Allah, Muhammad, and Ali.

A carved wooden panel in the Great Mosque at Xian, in China.

Sunnis

In most Muslim countries, the majority of people follow the Sunni branch of Islam. Its name comes from the Sunnah, which refers to the way of Muhammad, based on the Prophet's words or acts. The Sunni accept the first three caliphs (see page 13) as Muhammad's legitimate successors and are sometimes referred to as Orthodox Muslims.

Submission to Allah

The Arabic word Islam means "submission." The word derives from salam, meaning "peace," so to Arabic-speakers it suggests the peaceful state that comes from surrendering one's life to **Allah**, the only God. Muslims believe that the Islamic faith brings peace to those who live life in the way God intends.

8

The revelation

The holy book of Islam, the Qur'an (or "revelation"), expresses the word of God as it was revealed to the Prophet. **Arabic** was the language of revelation, and the Qur'an helped to spread Arabic as the common language of Muslims, which it remains to this day.

An amber and silver bead necklace from Yemen. The central bead can be opened to reveal holy words of the Qur'an.

Beautiful Arabic lettering, especially of texts from the Qur'an, became a major part of Islamic art.

Muslim culture

Medieval Muslims made many advances in science, technology, and scholarship. As Islam spread during the Middle Ages, it took Muslim culture with it. Ancient Greek and Roman texts were first translated into Arabic, which then itself became an international language of both literature and commerce.

The holiest city

Mecca, in modern Saudi Arabia, was the birthplace of Muhammad and is the world's holiest city for Muslims. It is the center of Islamic pilgrimage, and Muslims all over the world turn towards its focal point when they pray. That focus is the cube-shaped **Ka'bah** shrine, the most sacred spot for all Muslims. Every year millions of pilgrims visit the city, which is not open to non-Muslims.

The Ka'bah stands in the courtyard of the Great Mosque, in the heart of Mecca. It is covered with a black cloth.

Prayer

Praying to Allah is a very important part of worship for all Muslims. Muhammad established the call to prayer in 623 after he arrived in Medina. Ritual prayers, called **salah**, are performed five times a day (see page 15), and there is a special congregation for men on Friday. Muslims also say personal prayers, called *du'a*, in which they ask Allah for help or guidance.

The Dome of the Rock is Jerusalem's holiest Muslim shrine.

Jerusalem

Jerusalem was a holy city to Muhammad, and at first he told his companions to turn toward it when they prayed. He later changed the direction to Mecca. Muslims believe that Muhammad ascended to heaven during his "night journey" from Jerusalem in 619 (see page 12). Just six years after the Prophet's death, the city was conquered by Muslim forces. Today, most of the people living in east Jerusalem are Muslim Arabs.

Some Muslims use a string of 99 beads, separated into 3 groups of 33, to help them pray. They pass the prayer beads through their fingers, praising Allah as they touch each one.

Origins of Islam

The Arabs are first mentioned in Assyrian texts around 1,400 years before the birth of Muhammad. The term was used to refer to **nomadic** herders of northern Arabia and the Middle East, who were organized into various related tribes. They spoke Arabic, which belongs to the Semitic family of languages. Some Arabs began to settle in caravan towns and even developed small **city-states**. But many became nomads again when their towns were either invaded or caught in the conflict between the neighboring empires of the Byzantines and the Sassanids. The coming of Islam would bring the Arabs together as a powerful force.

Statue of the ancient Canaanite storm and weather god Baal, who was worshiped throughout the region.

Pre-Islamic religions

Before Muhammad, most Arabians worshiped local gods and goddesses. Some of these were tribal deities, while others were regional. In southern Arabia there were cults based on the stars and a moon god, showing the influence of the ancient Babylonians and Zoroastrianism. In cities and commercial centers, Jews and Christians succeeded in converting locals to the idea of a single God.

Two great empires ruled the region before the time of Muhammad. During the 6th century each had its greatest ruler: Emperor Justinian ruled the Byzantines, while King Khosrow reigned over the Sassanids.

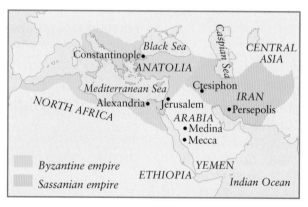

Between two empires

Sixth-century Arabia was caught between two great, opposing empires. To the northwest was the Byzantine empire, the name given to the Eastern Roman empire controlled from Constantinople. The Byzantines were Christians. To the east of Arabia was the Sassanian empire, run from Ctesiphon. The Sassanids were Zoroastrians.

The sky god Ahura Mazda (the "Wise Lord"), shown as a guardian spirit, with wings spread to protect the world.

Zoroastrianism

The Persian Zoroastrians followed the teachings of an ancient priest named Zoroaster, or Zarathustra, meaning "He of the golden light." The priest had seen a vision of a supreme god of goodness, light, and truth called Ahura Mazda. The god asked Zoroaster to fight against Angra Mainyu, the destructive force of greed and anger. Zoroastrians practiced animal sacrifice and an ancient fire cult.

This Persian illustration shows a magic tree that was worshiped by the Arabs in pre-Islamic times.

Arabian mythology

According to Arabian mythology, humans were made from clay and angels from light. The Arabians also believed in demons called jinn, who were intelligent beings created from smokeless flames. These demons were usually invisible, but they could suddenly appear in either human or animal form. They could be good or bad, and they appeared in many Arabian fables and folk tales.

Growth of Mecca

In ancient times Mecca was a settlement on the trade route between the southern Arabian peninsula and the Mediterranean Sea. A tradition of annual fairs grew up there, and because these included primitive forms of idol worship, the town became a place of pilgrimage. The first permanent houses were probably put up in the 5th century, and Mecca remained a center of commerce.

The Arabian camel, or dromedary, was first domesticated by nomadic Arab tribes around 1500 BCE. The camels were then taken along caravan routes to North Africa.

Ancient states

From about 500 BCE nomadic Arab tribes had established small states around cities on the caravan trade routes across the Middle Eastern deserts. The Nabateans settled in Petra, in modern Jordan, and other tribes developed the city of Palmyra, in present-day Syria. Both city-states were eventually taken over by the Romans.

This funerary statue comes from southern Arabia and dates from the 1st century BCE.

The *Romance of Antar*

Antarrah ibn-Shaddad, known as Antar, was a 6th-century Arab poet and warrior, who was celebrated in the later *Romance* as a model of chivalry in the desert. The son of a **Bedouin** chieftain and a slave girl, Antar showed his courage in many adventures that he undertook to win the hand of his beloved Ablah in marriage.

Merchants were important in Arabian society, and goods were transported for long distances along recognized trade routes. Mecca stood on such a route.

The Ka'bah

According to Arab legend, the ancient Meccan temple called the Ka'bah (meaning "cube") was built by Adam, the first man. It was the first house of God on earth, but was washed away by the great flood at the time of Noah. It was rebuilt by Ibrahim (Abraham) and his son Ismael, and Ibrahim placed inside it the **Black Stone** given to him by the angel Gabriel. By the time of Muhammad, there were more than 360 altars and idols in the Ka'bah.

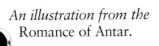

An illustration from the Romance of Antar.

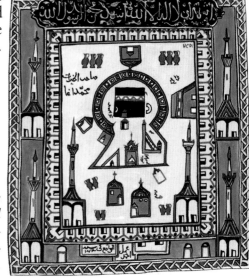

This tile from the tomb of Muhammad shows the black-shrouded, cube-shaped Ka'bah.

Muhammad's birth, shown in a 16th-century Ottoman miniature.

The Life of the Prophet

The Prophet Muhammad (570–632) was born in the town of Mecca, now in Saudi Arabia. As a boy he worked as a trader, having no formal education and probably never learning to read and write. He was 40 years old when he received his first revelation from Allah. When he was 52 he and his followers left Mecca for Medina, and this journey marks the beginning of the Islamic era. Muhammad fought against the Meccans for eight years, until they finally agreed to accept Islam, and Muhammad was able to destroy their pagan idols.

Birth of Muhammad

Muhammad was born in 570 CE. His parents belonged to the leading tribe of the Meccan region, the Quraish. His father died soon after he was born and, as was local custom, he was given to a Bedouin woman to bring up. When Muhammad was six, his real mother died, and he went first to live with his grandfather and then with his uncle, Abu Talib.

The first revelation

One night in 610, when Muhammad was 40 years old, he was praying in a cave on Mount Hira, near Mecca. Suddenly, he heard a voice calling his name, and the angel Gabriel appeared and told him that he was to be the messenger of God. Though Muhammad could not read the words that he was shown, he felt that they were written on his heart and he could recite them.

The first revelation was brought by the angel Gabriel in 610 CE. He continued to bring revelations until Muhammad's death.

The night journey

One night the angel Gabriel took Muhammad on a winged horse to the Temple of Jerusalem. From there the Prophet was taken to the seven heavens, where he met earlier Prophets, including Moses and Jesus. Then Muhammad went on alone to the highest heaven and the throne of Allah. The Prophet's followers later differed over whether this had been a bodily journey or a spiritual one.

Muhammad's followers

At first only Muhammad's first wife, Khadijah, and others very close to him heard and accepted the Prophet's message. When he began to preach the message openly, many people jeered at him. They were outraged that he wanted people to stop worshiping idols in the Ka'bah. Many of those who did believe him were persecuted.

Muhammad, whose face is not shown in this miniature, was often invited to dine with his early followers.

Muhammad's mosque and tomb in Medina, from a 16th-century Moroccan text.

Abu Bakr

The wealthy merchant Abu Bakr (left) was Muhammad's closest friend. He had total belief in the Prophet and became the first adult male Muslim. Muhammad later married Abu Bakr's daughter, Aishah. After the Prophet's death, Abu Bakr became the first caliph (from the Arabic for "successor"), leading the Muslim community from 632 to 634.

Aishah

Abu Bakr's daughter, the beautiful Aishah, was Muhammad's youngest wife. She accepted the simple life lived by Muhammad, and sometimes stood in prayer with him the whole night long. Aishah was kind and generous. She was also strong: in 656, she went into battle to avenge the murdered caliph Uthman. Today, many Muslims visit her room in Medina.

Muhammad lifts the sacred Black Stone from the blanket held by Meccan tribal leaders.

The Hegira

Some wealthy people in Mecca hated Muhammad for attacking their way of life. They feared they would lose money and power, so they plotted against him. Finally, in 622, the Prophet and his followers left Mecca and journeyed north to the town of Yathrib, later called Medina. This journey is known as the Hegira, and it was so important that 622 became the first year in the Muslim calendar.

Aisha kneels with Muhammad's daughter Fatima and his wife from the Makhzum tribe, Umma Salama. The three women's faces are veiled.

Muhammad's death

One day in 632, Muhammad went to the mosque in Medina, where Abu Bakr was leading prayers. Abu Bakr wanted the Prophet to take over, but he asked his father-in-law to continue. Muhammad was very sick. He returned home and lay down in Aishah's arms, where he died. He was buried at that very spot, and his tomb is a place of pilgrimage.

Muhammad's companions weep at his death.

The Black Stone

In 605, the Ka'bah shrine was damaged by a flood. The leaders of Mecca rebuilt it, but then argued about who had the right to replace the sacred Black Stone. They agreed to let Muhammad decide, and he allowed the tribal leaders to carry the stone together, on a blanket. He then put the stone in position himself, which satisfied everyone and earned him further trust.

The Basic Teachings of Islam

Muslims are guided by God's message as revealed through the holy book of the Qur'an. They also follow the hadiths, or sayings and traditions, handed down by the Prophet Muhammad. A set of commandments and laws known as the **shari'a,** meaning "path," shows Muslims how to lead good lives. In addition, all Muslims have special duties to perform. Known as the **Five Pillars of Islam,** the duties involve professing faith, praying, helping the needy, fasting, and pilgrimage.

The Qur'an

The holy book of the Qur'an, which means "revelation," is made up of 114 chapters. Muslims believe that it expresses precisely the word of God. Since it was compiled originally in Arabic, any translated version is thought to lose some of the intended spirit and meaning. The book itself is treated with great respect, and is often put on a stool-shaped bookrest for reading.

This open hand appears on the keystone of an arched doorway of the Alhambra palace in Granada, Spain. The five fingers represent the Pillars of Islam.

The Five Pillars

Each of the Five Pillars of Islam is a basic duty or requirement. Together, these essential duties support the whole structure of Islam, in the same way that stone pillars hold up a temple. Each pillar is an important part of the supporting structure, forming a firm foundation for Islam.

A beautifully inscribed and decorated page of a medieval Qur'an.

In this Moroccan panel embroidered in gold thread, the words of the shahadah form a human figure at prayer.

The afterlife

Muslims are taught that life on earth is a test, in which people's actions determine their places in the afterlife. When they die, the angel of death leads their souls to the day of judgement. Those who led a good life on earth are rewarded in paradise, which the Qur'an describes as a green garden full of trees and flowers. Those who fail the test go to hell.

This 15th-century miniature shows sinners enduring the fires of hell.

Shahadah

The first Pillar of Islam means "bearing witness." It is a declaration or profession of faith that there is only one God (Allah), and that Muhammad was his messenger. Muslims say the words of the shahadah first thing in the morning and last thing at night.

This compass can be used to find the direction of Mecca from wherever prayers are being said.

Salah

Salah, or ritual prayer, forms the second of the Five Pillars. The prayers must be said kneeling in the direction of the Ka'bah in Mecca. They are performed five times a day – just before sunrise, in the early afternoon, between mid-afternoon and sunset, in the evening after sunset, and between the hours of darkness and dawn. The times for salah are called by the muezzin at the mosque, but Muslims may pray at home.

Sawm

The fourth Pillar involves fasting from sunrise to sunset during the month of **Ramadan**. Healthy adult Muslims do not eat or drink anything between dawn and dusk. When Ramadan falls in the summer, these days of fasting are very long. Children under 12, pregnant and nursing mothers, old and sick people, as well as those on a journey, do not have to fast.

Zakah – charity money used to help the poor.

Zakah

Zakah, which means "cleansing," is a form of charity or welfare collection. It is the third Pillar of Islam. Today, Muslims see it as a duty to give two-and-a-half percent, or one fortieth, of their wealth to help others. In Muslim countries zakah is collected by the government, and elsewhere it is usually paid to a committee formed by the Muslim community.

Sharing

In addition to the duty of zakah (see above), Muslims help the homeless and others who are less fortunate than themselves. They may help them directly or make donations to charities such as Islamic Relief or the Red Crescent. In this way they show Allah how grateful they are for what they have. Wealthy Muslims have traditionally founded schools and hospitals, while others have provided public wells and fountains.

Children from Singapore put on special clothes to celebrate the end of the Ramadan fast.

Hajj

The fifth Pillar is **hajj** (see pages 28–29), a special pilgrimage to Mecca in the 12th month of the Islamic calendar. This annual pilgrimage brings together millions of Muslims from all over the world in common worship. Pilgrims wear simple clothes and make a special journey in and around Mecca. All Muslims must try to make the journey once in their lifetimes.

A 13th-century illustration of pilgrims traveling in a caravan to Mecca.

A public water fountain in Jerusalem.

Islam Expands

By the time Muhammad died in 632, Islam had conquered most of central and southern Arabia. In the hundred years following his death, Muslim Arabs conquered and converted the people of Mesopotamia, the Levant, North Africa, and parts of southern Spain and France. For almost six centuries Muslim rulers came from just two **dynasties**: the Umayyads, who made their capital in Damascus; and the Abbasids, who ruled from Baghdad.

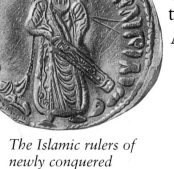

The Islamic rulers of newly conquered countries issued their own coinage. This coin (above) shows the Umayyad caliph, Abd al-Malik, holding the sword of Islam, a symbol of power.

The Umayyads

The Umayyad family, the first great dynasty of the Muslim empire, ruled from 661–750 CE. The Umayyad caliphate reached its peak under Abd al-Malik (reigned 685–705), when Arab armies overran most of Spain, invaded northern India, and conquered large areas of central Asia. Arabic was made the official language, financial administration was reorganized, and new Arab coinage introduced.

This mosaic comes from the court at Damascus, capital city of the Umayyads. It shows the Garden of Eden as described in the Qu'ran.

The Abbasids

In 750 CE, the Abbasids, who were descendants of Muhammad's uncle, overthrew the Umayyads. They moved the capital of the Muslim world to Baghdad. During the first 100 years of their reign, the power and prestige of the empire grew quickly and advances were made in industry, science, commerce, and the arts. The Abbasids ruled until 1258 when they were overthrown by the Mongols.

The great Abbasid caliph Harun al-Rashid reigned from 786 to 809. This illustration shows him in a Turkish bath, in an episode from the 1001 Nights.

Competing dynasties

The Abbasid dynasty was challenged by a number of rival Muslim dynasties. The Fatimids ruled in much of North Africa from 909 onward. The Seljuks, a Turkish tribe from central Asia, founded a large empire in western Asia. The Almoravids conquered the western part of North Africa and then crossed over into Spain.

This double-headed eagle represents the Seljuks, who overpowered the Abbasids in 1055. They respected the caliph's religious leadership and restored the dynasty's authority.

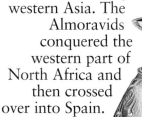

The Fatimids established a splendid court at Cairo after conquering Egypt in 969 CE. This crystal ewer was made in Cairo under Fatimid rule.

Muslim warriors

The Arab cavalry was mounted on fast Arabian horses, and well-armed with bows, spears, and sabers, the shape of which recalls the half-moon symbol of Islam. They wore coats of mail for protection, helmets with crests, and carried small round wooden or leather shields.

Charlemagne (Charles the Great), king of the Franks, fought in Spain against Muslim invaders in 778 CE. In this French miniature, the Islamic soldiers are shown as devils. Christians often referred to Muslims as infidels (unfaithful ones).

☐ Islamic conquests

☐ Byzantine empire

About 800, the Islamic world covered all of southwestern Asia, the coast of North Africa, the Mediterranean islands, and most of the Iberian peninsula.

SPAIN
Cordoba •
Seville •
ITALY
Rome •
NORTH AFRICA
Mediterranean Sea
Black Sea
Constantinople •
Damascus •
SYRIA
• Jerusalem
• Baghdad
AFGHANISTAN
• Samarkand
Al-Fusat •
PALESTINE
ARABIA
• Medina
• Mecca
Indian Ocean

This huge vase (right) dates from the time of the Nasrid dynasty in Granada, the last of the Muslim dynasties in Spain.

The Crusades

For a period of almost 200 years, from 1095 until 1291, the Christian popes and kings of Europe mounted ferocious military attacks on the Muslim rulers who controlled Jerusalem and other places associated with the earthly life of Christ. The knights of the First Crusade conquered Jerusalem in 1099. They were expelled again by the great Muslim leader Saladin in 1187. The Mamelukes had repulsed the last of the Crusaders by the end of the 13th century.

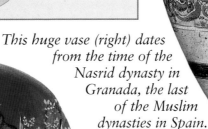

Islamic Spain

The first Muslim armies entered Spain in the early 8th century CE. By the end of that century, they had control of most of the Iberian peninsula (modern Spain and Portugal). Several Muslim dynasties ruled over magnificent courts until the Arabs were finally expelled in 1492. The Umayyad dynasty in Andalusia (founded by a survivor of the Umayyads in Arabia) marked the zenith of Arabic civilization in Spain. Later dynasties included the Almoravids, the Almohads, and the Nasrids.

Science and Knowledge

Early Islamic scientists and scholars were greatly influenced by the works of the ancient Persians and Indians, and most of all by those of the ancient Greeks. Muslim scholars copied and translated many Greek manuscripts, which ultimately benefited the whole world, since otherwise many of the ancient texts might have been lost during the European Middle Ages. Arabic became the leading language of science, and Muslim scientists such as al-Khwarizmi and ibn-Sina (known as Avicenna) wrote works that influenced the rest of the world.

The ideas of the ancient Greek philosopher and scientist Aristotle, who was known as the "first teacher," had great influence in the Islamic world. This portrait of him comes from a 13th-century Muslim manuscript.

Technology

Muslim scientists made great strides in technology and engineering. An engineer named al-Jazari, who worked at the beginning of the 13th century, invented a whole range of machines and included them in his *Book of Knowledge of Mechanical Devices*. They included water-lifting machines and clocks.

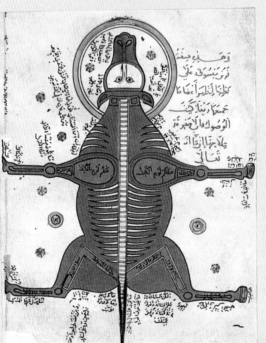

As well as human anatomy, Islamic medical scientists studied animals. This illustration from a 15th-century Egyptian text shows the skeleton of a horse.

Medicine

Medieval Islamic physicians based their work on ancient Greek and Roman medicine. A Persian named Muhammad al-Razi (865–923), known as Rhazes, was the greatest physician of his age. He studied the kidneys and other organs, recorded diseases such as smallpox and measles, and noted all his findings for other doctors to use. He also wrote an enormous encyclopedia of medicine, pointing out errors made by the ancient Greeks.

This illustration from al-Jazari's book shows a candle clock. A figure popped out of a door each time an hour passed.

This 13th-century illustration shows a Muslim pharmacist preparing drugs.

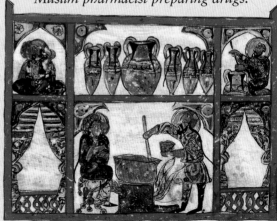

Hospitals and medical schools

The first hospital was opened in Baghdad in the 9th century, and a century later there were four more hospitals in the city. Others were built in Mecca, Medina, Cairo, and Damascus, and the medical care they provided was available to everyone. Doctors from all over the Muslim world came to these hospitals to practice and learn. In the 13th century a special school of medicine opened in Damascus.

١ ٢ ٣ ٤ ٥ ٦ ٧ ٨ ٩ ٠
1 2 3 4 5 6 7 8 9 0

Arabic numerals included a dot for zero.

Arabic numerals
Before Islam the Arabs used a system known as finger reckoning, in which numbers were written out in words. This was fine for simple arithmetic but not very good for multiplication and division. Later Muslim travelers and traders adopted the Hindu system, which used nine digits and a zero. Among the Muslims these were known as "Indian numerals," but when they brought them to Europe, they became known as Arabic numerals.

Algebra
Muslims made great developments in this branch of mathematics, which had been used in an earlier form by the ancient Egyptians and Babylonians. In the 9th century a Persian mathematician named Muhammad al-Khwarizmi (c.800–850) wrote a book on **algebra**, and the word itself comes from part of the Arabic title of this work, al-jabr, meaning "restoration."

A page from al-Khwarizmi's book, which was later translated into Latin and introduced algebra to Europe.

Geography
By the 12th century Muslims had knowledge of the basic outlines of Asia, North Africa, and Europe. The great Moroccan geographer al-Idrisi (c.1100–66) traveled widely before settling at the court of Roger II of Sicily, who asked him to produce a map of the world. The result (right, with north at the bottom) was remarkably accurate for the time.

By the 16th century Muslim astronomers had great knowledge and a wide variety of instruments. This illustration shows astronomers working in an observatory built in Istanbul in 1575.

This 13th-century miniature shows a library in Baghdad. The shelves are stacked with books.

Scholarship
Muslims built schools all over the Islamic world. Special schools called kuttabs were attached to mosques, where boys learned about the Qur'an and other things. The al-Azhar Mosque was founded in Cairo in about 970, and its school grew into a university with free tuition. This was probably the first university in the world.

Astronomy
In the 8th century Muslim scholars translated Indian and Persian astronomical works into Arabic, and a century later they also translated the ancient Greek scholar Ptolemy's works. Muslims built on earlier ideas, and one of their greatest achievements was to develop and improve the astrolabe. They used this instrument both to find their way across the desert and to determine the direction of Mecca.

Islam in Africa

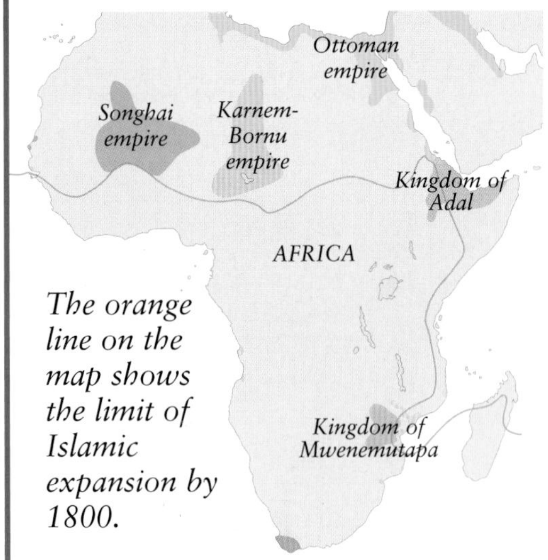

Soon after the death of Muhammad in the 7th century, Muslims conquered large parts of northern Africa and introduced Islam. They spread around the fringes of the Sahara Desert, later trading with several kingdoms that flourished in the Niger valley of western Africa. Over the centuries the large kingdoms of Ghana, Mali, and Songhai became centers of Muslim learning. The religious and cultural traditions lived on in the region, and today Islam is still the dominant faith in the north and much of the center of the continent.

The orange line on the map shows the limit of Islamic expansion by 1800.

Map labels: Ottoman empire, Songhai empire, Karnem-Bornu empire, Kingdom of Adal, AFRICA, Kingdom of Mwenemutapa

Islam arrives

By 640 Muslim soldiers and settlers had spread from the Arabian peninsula to Egypt. Two years later Alexandria fell to the Arabs, who continued southward up the Nile Valley toward present-day Sudan, as well as westward across the edge of the Sahara Desert. In 698 the ancient city of Carthage fell to the Muslims. Then, at the beginning of the 8th century, the Berbers – who had lived near the Mediterranean coast of North Africa for thousands of years – also accepted Islam.

These prayer beads from western Sudan (below) were a souvenir of an African pilgrim's visit to Mecca.

Songhai empire

By the 15th century the trading state of the Songhai people, who had adopted Islam, was the most powerful empire in West Africa. This dominance was achieved under King Sunni Ali (ruled 1464–92, above), whose army overran the trading centers of Timbuktu and Djenné. The later King Askia Muhammad (ruled 1493–1538) further encouraged the practice of Islam among his people. The Songhai empire was defeated by a Moroccan army in 1591.

Mansa Musa receives an Arab trader at his court.

Mansa Musa

Mansa Musa (above) was emperor of the West African empire of Mali from 1307 to 1332. He is best remembered for his magnificent pilgrimage to Mecca – a journey of about 4,400 miles (7,000 km) – which he undertook in 1324. The emperor rode on horseback and was accompanied by 60,000 men, with a baggage train of 80 camels laden with gold. In Mali, Mansa Musa had many mosques built, introduced public prayer, and developed Islamic scholarship.

Pilgrimage

African Muslims try to make a pilgrimage to Mecca once in their lives. As Islam spread throughout the continent, central and west African rulers made the hajj, visiting Egypt on the way. In the 16th century the Songhai King Askia Muhammad stopped at Cairo on his way to Mecca and was given the title of caliph by the Abbasid ruler in Egypt. Scholars from Timbuktu made the same journey and learned many things from the Egyptians.

Mud-brick mosques

From the 14th century many African mosques were built using sun-dried mud bricks. These were placed around a wooden framework, making it easy to repair the walls after heavy rainfall or any other damage. Two of the most famous mud-brick mosques are in the cities of Djenné and Mopti, in Mali, where 90 percent of the population is Muslim.

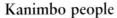

Djenné was founded in the 13th century and quickly grew as a trading city. Today's large mud-brick building was built in the traditional style on the foundations of an earlier mosque.

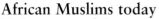

The religious leader of the Kanimbo people, called the Grand Malam, leads communal prayer in the desert of northern Chad.

Kanimbo people

The Kanimbo, or Kanembu, of northern Chad are descendants of an empire that lasted from the 8th to the 19th century. The Kanem-Bornu empire surrounded Lake Chad, and its rulers converted to Islam in 1086. The empire grew rich from trade in copper, salt, and horses, which were exchanged for ivory and kola nuts from the south. Today, more than half of the people of Chad are Muslim.

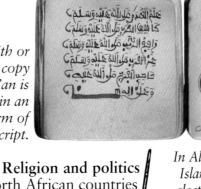

This small 17th or 18th-century copy of the Qur'an is written in an African form of Arabic script.

African Muslims today

Today most of the countries of the northern half of the continent, including all those with Mediterranean coasts, have Muslim majorities. Islam stretches across northern Africa, from Senegal on the Atlantic coast (where 94 percent of people follow Islam) to Somalia (where almost the entire population is Muslim) and the Indian Ocean. The continent's largest Islamic populations live in Egypt, Nigeria, and Algeria.

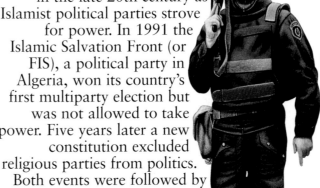

A young Senegalese boy learns about Islam.

Religion and politics

In many North African countries Islam is the state religion established by law. In several of these countries problems arose in the late 20th century as Islamist political parties strove for power. In 1991 the Islamic Salvation Front (or FIS), a political party in Algeria, won its country's first multiparty election but was not allowed to take power. Five years later a new constitution excluded religious parties from politics. Both events were followed by unrest and extreme violence.

In Algeria, when the Islamists won the elections the military stopped them from taking power.

Worship

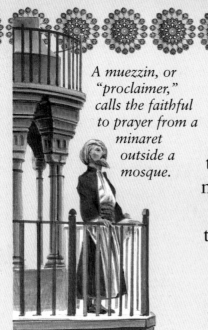

A muezzin, or "proclaimer," calls the faithful to prayer from a minaret outside a mosque.

Worship is an extremely important aspect of Islam, and Muslims believe that praying five times a day adds structure to their lives. They pray at home or in a mosque. Worshipers make special physical movements, which are intended to help them devote themselves to prayer, focusing the mind so that they think of nothing else. Prayers last only a few minutes on each of the five occasions. On Fridays, men meet together in a special congregation for their midday prayers, and in Muslim countries all shops and businesses close at that time.

Preparation for prayer

Muslims must prepare for their prayers. First they put everything else out of their minds and concentrate fully on Allah. Then they wash themselves in a ritual called wudu. They wash their hands, rinse their mouths and nostrils, then wash their faces, arms, heads, and feet. If no water is available, they perform a symbolic wash. In the desert they do this with sand.

Standing for prayer

There is a series of set movements for salah, which includes four basic positions. During the first of these, called qiyam ("standing"), the worshiper places the right hand lightly over the left. Some Muslim groups hold their hands by their thighs instead. In this position the worshiper recites the opening chapter of the Qur'an.

Bowing

The opening is followed by a deep bow, during which the worshipers place their hands on their knees. They recite three times, in Arabic, "Glory be to my great God." By bowing low, they show respect and love for Allah. This and all the other prayer positions are performed in the direction of Mecca.

Prostration

Worshipers get down on their knees and then prostrate themselves, showing complete readiness to do whatever Allah wants them to do. They touch the ground with their foreheads and noses, and the palms of their hands and fingers lie flat and point toward Mecca. They say three times, "Glory be to my God, the greatest of the great."

Kneeling

Worshipers return to the kneeling position, in which they sit on their feet and place their hands on their knees. This is the posture of a humble slave, and they say three times, "Master, forgive me." Finally, they turn their heads to the right and left, asking Allah to bless all other worshipers. The complete sequence is repeated several times.

This 16th-century Persian illustration shows young Muslims studying the Qur'an with their teacher.

Learning the Qur'an

Muslims are taught to recite the Qur'an. Children throughout the Islamic world are taught the Arabic alphabet and then learn how to pronounce the Qur'anic words and phrases correctly. Many men and women learn all the chapters of the holy book by heart. A person who does this is called a hafiz. Studying, reciting, and learning the Qur'an are important to all Muslims.

The first mosque

The word mosque comes from the Arabic word masjid, which means "place of prostration." The first mosque was built by Muhammad and his companions just after his arrival in Medina in 622. It was a large enclosure with mud-brick walls, with an open portico at one end made of palm-trunk columns and a roof of leaves and mud. There were huts for the Prophet and his family outside one wall, with entrances into the courtyard.

Prayer mats

The place where a Muslim prays must be clean. Worshipers do not have to use mats to kneel on, but some Muslims have favorite prayer mats that they keep at home. A mat may be a woolen carpet, or it may be made of cotton or straw. Prayer mats often have geometric patterns, or sometimes pictures of famous mosques, but they never show images of people.

This prayer mat was made of wool and silk in the 17th century, during the reign of the Mogul emperors in India.

This Turkish miniature shows the building of an early mosque.

Inside a mosque

All mosques provide a clean space and an indication of the direction of Mecca. The prayer hall is spacious and airy. An arched niche, called a **mihrab**, is set in the wall opposite the entrance, and when worshipers face this, they know they are facing Mecca. The mihrab is often finely decorated. To the right of it is a minbar, or pulpit, from which sermons are delivered.

The Great Mosque of Damascus

This is the world's oldest surviving stone mosque. It was completed in 715, when Damascus was the capital of the Umayyad empire. The building was originally a Christian church, and it contains a shrine which supposedly contains the head of St. John the Baptist. The mosque has a large prayer hall and an enormous open courtyard surrounded by an arcade of arches. It became the model for many mosques throughout the Islamic world.

The main entrance of the Great Mosque has mosaics of a beautiful landscape above the arches.

Islam in Asia

Islam moved south into the Indian subcontinent in 711, when Arab invaders conquered the kingdom of Sind at the mouth of the River Indus. Further raids were led by the Ghaznavids in the year 1000, and power eventually moved to the growing city of Delhi. The Delhi **sultanate** was finally overthrown in the 16th century by other Muslims when they established the Mogul empire. By that time Islam had been taken to Southeast Asia by traders using the summer monsoon winds to sail from the Bay of Bengal to the South China Sea. Islam has remained the leading religion in the regions which became Pakistan, Bangladesh, Indonesia, and Malaysia.

Mahmud was a patron of the arts. The illustration shows him listening to poetry at his court.

This miniature from a 14th-century manuscript illustrates a traditional Muslim story in a typically Hindu style.

Mahmud of Ghazna

In the year 1000, Mahmud of Ghazna (971–1030) launched the first of 17 invasions into India. Mahmud was the third sultan of the Ghaznavid dynasty, which ruled a kingdom in what is now Afghanistan. His army consisted mainly of Turkish slaves who had previously served Persian rulers. Mahmud filled his court with scholars, scientists, and linguists.

Muslims and Hindus

In 1200 Muhammad of Gaur, a Muslim from Afghanistan like Mahmud of Ghazna before him, overcame Hindu resistance and conquered the plains beside the two great rivers, the Indus to the west and the Ganges to the east. Although Muslims and Hindus fought over territory for centuries, however, their cultures and traditions often intermingled successfully.

The Delhi sultanate

After the death of Muhammad of Gaur, a Turkish slave general named Qutb-ud-din Aibak founded an independent Muslim sultanate in the small fortress town of Delhi. The town soon grew into a city that was to be at the center of Indian politics for hundreds of years. At its largest, the Delhi sultanate stretched all the way from Sind (in modern Pakistan) to Bengal (in modern India and Bangladesh).

Technology

Islamic influence in the Indian subcontinent included technological developments, many of which were brought south from Muslim-controlled Persia. Irrigation had been practiced in India for hundreds of years, but Muslims brought their own advanced form of wheel irrigation, using camels (above).

The Muslims also introduced paper, gunpowder, and the true arch to India.

The 240-foot-(73 m) high Qutb Minar minaret was built of local sandstone beside a mosque in Delhi. The mosque itself, begun in 1199, was built on an earlier Hindu temple site.

Malaysia and Indonesia

From 1295, Samudra – on the northern coast of Sumatra – became an important center for the spread of Islam. We know from the written records of travelers that several Muslim communities flourished on Sumatra by the middle of the 14th century. The city-state of Melaka was soon to extend its influence to Sumatra and other Indonesian islands.

Sailing from India

By the 14th century the Strait of Malacca, between the Malayan peninsula and the island of Sumatra (in present-day Indonesia), had become a major sea route for traders sailing between India and China. The city of Melaka was founded around 1400 and soon became the most important port in Southeast Asia. The city-state's ruler, the Malay prince Paramesvara, converted to Islam in 1413.

A mosque at Kuala Kangsar, in northwest Malaysia.

Malaysian children study the Qur'an. Today, more than half the population of Malaysia is Muslim, and the great majority of Indonesians follow Islam.

Borneo

After Islam had reached the island of Borneo, to the east of Sumatra, the state of Brunei assumed control of the north coast. Today, Borneo is shared between three countries – Malaysia, Indonesia, and the small state of Brunei, which is a sultanate. The sultan is the head of state and is one of the richest people in the world because of his country's large reserves of oil and natural gas.

Java

As on the other islands of Southeast Asia, there were many different kingdoms on Java when Muslims first arrived around 1400. The Javanese kingdom of Majapahit was taken over by an Islamic conquest in 1478, but regional courts and customs remained on the island. The building of the mosque at the central city of Yogyakarta was started by Sultan Agung early in the 17th century, but was only completed more than a hundred years later.

This illustration shows Dipanegara, the Muslim leader who led the holy war against the Javanese aristocracy and then against the Dutch colonizers. He was important in introducing Islam to Java.

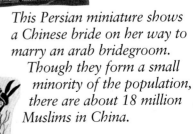

This Persian miniature shows a Chinese bride on her way to marry an arab bridegroom. Though they form a small minority of the population, there are about 18 million Muslims in China.

The Sufis

Sufis are Muslim mystics who search for a close, personal relationship with Allah. Their name comes from suf, the Arabic word for "wool," and refers to the simple woolen robes that the mystics used to wear. The Sufis are not a separate sect, and they can belong to the Sunni or Shi'ite branch of Islam, but there are different Sufi brotherhoods following their own shaikh, or spiritual teacher. Many groups sprang up in the 12th century, and they helped to spread Islam. Many of the greatest Muslim poets have been Sufis.

The whirling of the Dervishes is said to represent the rotation of the Earth and other planets around the Sun.

Music and dance
Unlike other Muslim groups, Sufis use music and dance as a way of reaching a higher level of consciousness. They play instruments such as the tambourine (left) and pipes to create a steady rhythm. A group known as Dervishes (a name which comes from the Persian for "beggars") whirl themselves into a trance so that they can become one with Allah.

An 18th-century Bengali illustration of Khwaja Khidr, who is thought to help those in danger of drowning.

Pre-Islamic cults
The early Sufis knew hundreds of ancient tales from pre-Islamic times. They kept the tales and their characters alive by reciting them and writing them down, and in this way earlier cults were included in Muslim traditions. One example was the cult of Khwaja Khidr, who first appeared in the *Epic of Gilgamesh*, which was composed in southern Mesopotamia before 2000 BC. From northern India to Turkey, this figure was associated with springtime, fertility, and happiness.

The elephant story comes from the Mathnawi, a poem written by the 13th-century Sufi mystic Jalal al-Rumi (see opposite).

*A 15th-century illustration of a **simurgh** poem written two centuries earlier.*

Animal symbols
Sufi poets have used both real and mythical animals as symbols in their work. The mother elephant (above) represented judgement when she sniffed out and killed some greedy men who had eaten her calf, which stood for righteousness. The mythical simurgh bird stood for the Sufis' wish to become one with the divine. When a flock of birds went on a hazardous journey to their king, called Simurgh, those who survived discovered that they were simurghs themselves.

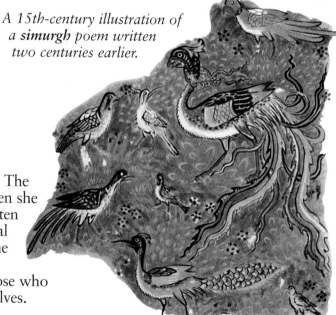

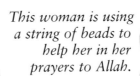

This 16th-century illustration tells the miraculous story of a cow bowing down at the sight of the great Sufi poet, al-Rumi.

This woman is using a string of beads to help her in her prayers to Allah.

Great poets

Many Sufi mystics have also been great poets and have influenced the whole of Islam through their work. One such was Jalal al-Rumi (1207–73). He lived in the town of Konya, not far from the Mediterranean coast of present-day Turkey. His son began having visions at the age of six, and later founded the order of the Mevlevi, or Whirling Dervishes.

Begging

For many, Sufism involved giving up worldly possessions and taking vows of poverty. This meant that they had to beg in order to live. This 15th-century illustration (left) shows a Sufi beggar wearing an animal skin.

Female mystics

In the Sufi tradition, women can also have mystical experiences, and two famous mystics were women. Sayyida Nafisah (died 824), who was famous for her learning and devotion, was a direct descendant of Muhammad's grandson Hasan. Rabi'a al-Adawiyya (721–801) was a slave girl who went on to devote her life to Allah, writing famous poems about her love of God.

Tombs and shrines

The tombs and shrines of important Sufis became places of pilgrimage and remain so today. An example is the tomb of the Persian Sufi Abdallah al-Ansari, who died in 1089. The tomb was built four centuries later near Herat, in modern Afghanistan. The illustration (left) shows part of the beautiful ceramic decoration of al-Ansari's tomb.

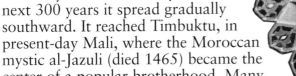

Mu'in al-Din Chishti's white marble tomb in Ajmer, northern India. Every year the anniversary of his death is remembered by the local Sufi community.

Africa

Sufism had great influence in North Africa by the 12th century. Over the next 300 years it spread gradually southward. It reached Timbuktu, in present-day Mali, where the Moroccan mystic al-Jazuli (died 1465) became the center of a popular brotherhood. Many copies of al-Jazuli's book of prayers (below) reached the region, and the prayers were eagerly recited. The leading scholars of Timbuktu were Sufis, despite the fact that many members of their families were leading merchants.

Chishti brotherhood

Sufism reached northern India in the 13th century, taken there by members of a brotherhood from Chisht, in modern Afghanistan. Mu'in al-Din (died c.1233) actually came from Sistan, in present-day Iran, but he traveled widely and took the name Chishti. He journeyed to Delhi, where he and other members of his brotherhood gained acceptance by their tolerance of local Hindu customs.

The Hajj

Every Muslim who is able must go on a special pilgrimage to Mecca, called the hajj. This must be done between the 8th and 13th of the month of Dhu'l-Hijjah. It used to take Muslims from faraway lands months or even years to reach Mecca, but today most fly in to Jeddah airport, about 44 miles (70 km) from Mecca. The millions of Muslims from different countries who go on the hajj each year feel a great sense of togetherness. Some save for years in order to be able to go, and sometimes families are able to send just one representative.

Male pilgrims must wear two sheets of plain white cloth. Women wear plain, loose dresses, leaving only their faces and hands bare.

This 13th-century earthenware tablet shows the month of pilgrimage, Dhu'l-Hijjah, the twelfth month in the Muslim calendar.

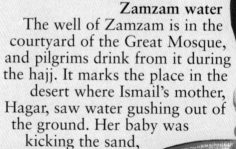

Many pilgrims take home water from the Zamzam well, so that they can share it with family and friends.

The pilgrimage includes a round journey on foot from the Great Mosque in Mecca.

Pilgrimage route
Pilgrims go first to Mecca's Great Mosque (1) and go around the Ka'bah (2) seven times in an anti-clockwise direction. They walk to Mina (3) and then stand at the plain of Arafat (4), near the Mount of Mercy (5). They spend the night at a tented camp (6), and return via Muzdalifah (7), where they pick up stones to throw at the pillars of Mina.

Zamzam water
The well of Zamzam is in the courtyard of the Great Mosque, and pilgrims drink from it during the hajj. It marks the place in the desert where Ismail's mother, Hagar, saw water gushing out of the ground. Her baby was kicking the sand, and Hagar said, "Zam zam" ("Stop, stop") and put stones around the well.

Stoning of Satan

The stone pillars at Mina represent the place where Ibrahim and Ismail were tempted by Satan to disobey God and threw stones at him to drive him away. On their way back to Mecca, pilgrims remember this by doing the same and throwing small stones at the pillars (below). In this way they show that they too are driving the devil away.

Mount Arafat

Hajj pilgrims gather on the plain that leads to Arafat, the Mount of Mercy, where Muhammad gave his last sermon in 632. They stay there from noon to sunset meditating, praying, and worshiping Allah. Pilgrims may listen to a sermon on the mountain (above). This is a most important part of the pilgrimage, and Muslims find it a great mystical experience.

Today, pilgrims buy coupons that corresponds to sacrificial rams.

The Feast of Sacrifice

On the tenth day of Dhu'l-Hijjah the Feast of Sacrifice begins and every pilgrim must sacrifice an animal. This commemorates the sacrifice that Ibrahim was prepared to make by killing his son Ismail. At the last moment, God stopped Ibrahim and a ram was sacrificed instead. When the animals are slaughtered in Mecca today, some meat is given to the poor and the rest is frozen for later use.

This 12th-century fragment certifies that a pilgrim had made the long journey to Mecca and Medina.

Hajji and hajjah

A man who has completed the hajj pilgrimage is known as a hajji, and a woman is called a hajjah. Pilgrims are understandably proud of having completed the hajj, but the Qur'an makes it clear that Muslims should only go if they are healthy, can provide for the families they leave behind, and can afford to make the pilgrimage. For those who cannot go, it is the intention that counts.

This family has painted pictures of its pilgrimage around its doorway.

The Muslim Empires

In the early 16th century four powers were established in the area of Islam comprising west and south Asia. They were the Ottomans in Turkey and the Near East, the Safavids in Iran (Persia), the Mughals in India, and the much smaller federation of the Uzbeks in Turkistan. The first three were especially strong powers. Their great cities, such as Istanbul, Isfahan, and Agra, showed their wealth and culture. The Ottomans, the greatest military power, penetrated deep into Europe, attacking Vienna, capital of the Holy Roman Empire. Some Europeans felt that their whole continent was in danger of being conquered. But by the 18th century, all the Muslim empires had faded. The Ottomans had been driven back to southeastern Europe. The Safavids had been overthrown. Mughal rule in India was breaking down, and Uzbekistan had split into separate states, or **khanates**.

Osman I (c.1258–1326) founded a small Turkish state in present-day Turkey. This gradually expanded to become the Ottoman empire.

The Ottomans

The Ottoman empire reached the height of its extent and power under the rule of its greatest sultan, Suleiman the Magnificent (left), during the first half of the 16th century. Its territories, encompassing much of North Africa, southwest Asia, and the Balkans, were held by a disciplined army. The capital, Istanbul, prospered with merchants coming from all over the world to buy and sell goods there, and the empire was crisscrossed with trade routes.

The great conquering dynasties were the Ottoman Turks, who expanded into Europe and North Africa, and the Mughals, who conquered India.

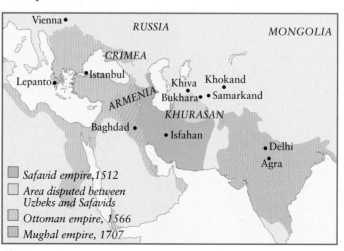

Conquering dynasties

The Muslim empires' rulers had much in common. They were all descended from nomadic Turkic or Mongol tribes. They all belonged to Islam, and educated men all spoke the language of Islam, Arabic. Persian was also spoken – and written by poets – in the Mughal and Ottoman courts, as well as in Iran.

Map labels:
Vienna • RUSSIA MONGOLIA
CRIMEA
Lepanto • Istanbul — Khiva • Khokand
ARMENIA Bukhara • Samarkand
KHURASAN
Baghdad • Isfahan •
Delhi •
Agra •

- Safavid empire, 1512
- Area disputed between Uzbeks and Safavids
- Ottoman empire, 1566
- Mughal empire, 1707

In 1529, under Suleiman the Magnificent, the Turks unsuccessfully besieged Vienna, capital of the Habsburg empire. In 1683 they gathered a huge army for another assault on the city, but were beaten again.

The Uzbeks

The Uzbek khans, like the Mughals, were descended from Chingis Khan and Tamerlane. About 1500 they formed the Uzbek tribes into a confederation. They fought with the Safavids over possession of Khurasan, a rich province, and also clashed with the Mughals. But they never created a centrally governed empire, and in the 17th century the region split up into separate khanates.

Statue of Tamerlane (also known as Timur).

Samarkand, the city of Tamerlane, was one of many fine religious and cultural centers of central Asia ruled by the Uzbek khans, who were strict Sunni Muslims.

The Safavids

The Safavid dynasty reached its peak under Shah Abbas (reigned 1588–1628). His reorganized army drove out the Uzbeks, regained land lost to the Ottomans, and captured Baghdad. He also encouraged local industry and export trade, run mainly by Armenian merchants who received special protection from the **Shah**. At Isfahan, his capital, he built a fantastic array of mosques, madrasas (religious colleges), and palaces.

Abbas the Great, a ruler of great energy and vision, built the beautiful city of Isfahan.

The Mughals

The Mughal empire was founded by Babur in 1526, but Mughal control was not firmly established until the reign of his grandson, Akbar (right). The greatest of the Mughals, Akbar was unique in practicing religious toleration – an unthinkable policy anywhere else in the world of Islam or in Christian Europe at that time.

Babur, founder of the Mughal empire, reading poetry.

Sharing a religion did not prevent conflict in Islam, especially between the Shi'ite Safavids and the Sunni Ottomans.

Decline of the Muslim empires

In the 17th century, the power of Islam was in decline. Poor government, costly wars, and inflation undermined the Ottoman empire which, after over a century of expansion, was forced onto the defensive. After Abbas the Great, the Safavids again began to lose their grip on Iran. All the Muslim empires faced increasing rebellions among their subjects.

After Suleiman, Ottoman sultans worked little in running their empires. They led luxurious lives in their courts. This led to weak government and the decline of their empires.

Islamic Art

The early Arab Muslims had little art of their own, but as they spread and conquered other lands, they adopted new cultural influences. These came together to form a distinctive style of art and architecture. The style was greatly affected by a restriction on painting or carving images of living things, including people. The Islamic religious authorities believed that if artists created such images, they would be imitating God. They also feared that people might worship them. Artists developed wonderful geometric designs, which became characteristic of all Islamic art.

This octagonal silver dish, dating from the 9th or 10th century, has roundels with the mythical simurgh bird.

Design motifs

In Islamic art the same techniques and designs are often used on different materials. A design motif that was originally developed for textiles, for example, might then be used on metalware, pottery, and glassware, or even in architecture. This was also true of the arabesque – scrollwork ornamentation consisting of winding stems and abstract leaves – that spread throughout the Islamic world from the 10th century.

A traditional Islamic scribe at work.

Books

Books have always played an important role in Islamic culture. Manuscripts of the Qur'an were beautifully written and decorated with graceful scrolls and floral decorations.

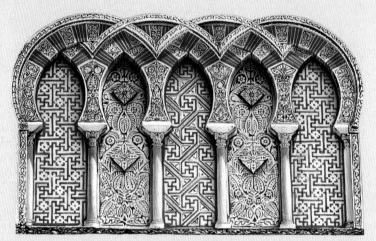

Rich, geometric decoration on the wall above the West Gate of the Great Mosque in Cordoba, Spain.

Religious architecture

The main feature of Persian and Turkish mosques was a large dome. Many North African and Spanish mosques were covered with beautiful tiles. The roof of the Great Mosque in Cordoba, Spain, was supported by more than a thousand arched pillars of granite, jasper, and marble. Later mosques, such as the Blue Mosque in Istanbul, became even more complex, with many domes and minarets.

The ceremonial signature of the Ottoman sultan Suleiman the Magnificent (c.1494–1566).

Calligraphy

Calligraphy, the art of beautiful writing, is an important feature of Islamic art. Arabic letters, which are written and read from right to left, were inscribed in several kinds of script. The Kufic script (right), originally from the town of Kufah in Iraq, is straight and geometric. Neskhi is more rounded, while Nastaliq is slanted.

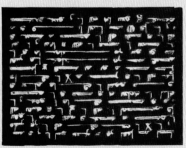

This sacred Islamic text from the 9th century is written in Kufic script.

The first Islamic coins were minted in the 7th century. The two sides of a gold dinar minted in 696, during the rule of the Umayyad caliph Abd al-Malik.

Metalwork

Since the Islamic religious authorities frowned on the use of precious metals for making metal goods, craftsmen worked mainly with bronze and brass. They engraved or embossed the metal, sometimes using gold, silver, or copper to inlay inscriptions or designs. Mosul, a town in modern Iraq near the Turkish border, became an important metalworking center. Metal goods became trading items for Muslims.

A 10th or 11th century incense burner from Persia.

This elaborately carved container from Cordoba dates from 968 AD, and shows two men listening to the music of a lute.

This ceramic mosque lamp was made during the reign of Suleiman the Magnificent.

Ceramics

Islamic potters developed their own techniques from about the 9th century. They engraved or painted pottery before adding glazes of many colors. In the Middle East and Spain, they then began painting with a metallic pigment on a blue or white shiny glaze, to produce pottery known as lusterware. They used similar glazing techniques for the tiles and mosaics with which they decorated mosques.

Mogul art

A special style developed under the patronage of the Mogul emperors of northern India during the 16th century. Originally the style owed much to earlier Persian art. The Moguls were masters of color, using different colored stones in their buildings. Polished white marble was used to reflect light, while red sandstone had the opposite effect. Precious stones, such as topaz and carnelian, were inlaid to add a jewel-like quality.

White marble is inlaid with semiprecious colored stones in this panel from an audience chamber in the Red Fort at Delhi. The sandstone palace was built by the Moguls between 1638 and 1648.

The Taj Mahal, near the north Indian city of Agra, took more than 20,000 workers about 18 years to build. It was completed in 1853 as a tomb for the wife of Shah Jahan, the Mogul emperor.

Palaces and tombs

The early Muslim caliphs built stone palaces in the desert, with thick walls and tall towers. Later domed palaces were built of bricks covered with thick layers of stucco. Few of these remain. The most famous remaining Muslim palaces are those built by the Moors in Spain and the Moguls in India. The 14th-century Alhambra palace, standing above the city of Granada, contains sunny courtyards surrounded by shady arcades. As well as palaces, the Moguls built huge, lavish tombs.

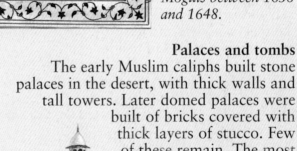

Emergence of Muslim States

During the 17th and 18th centuries the great powers of the Muslim world, including the Mughal, Ottoman, and Safavid empires, declined. They were challenged both by internal weaknesses, and the loss of wars and territory to the rising European powers. From the 17th century until the early part of the 20th century, European countries colonized many parts of the Muslim world. However, from the 1920s onward, the countries of the Middle East and Asia gradually reclaimed their independence and the modern Muslim states we know today came into being.

This illustration shows the Ottoman sultan Abdul Hamid II (ruled 1876–1909) fuming helplessly as Bosnia-Herzegovina goes to Austria-Hungary and Bulgaria becomes independent.

Decline of the Ottoman empire
During the 19th century the Ottoman empire became smaller and weaker. Several sultans tried to reform and modernize their state, including Selim III (shown above), who tried to modernize the army. They were defeated by opposition from within the empire as well as by interference from the European powers and Russia.

European expansion
The European colonial powers expanded ruthlessly, colonizing large parts of Asia and the Middle East, and almost all of Africa. Not only did they win wars and territory, but the European model of politics and society was copied by many Muslim leaders who tried to modernize their states, often to protect themselves from the Europeans.

Egypt
Mehemet Ali (1769–1849, left) was the Ottoman viceroy of Egypt from 1805 until 1848. He modernized Egypt along European lines. The British occupied Egypt in 1882 after suppressing an Arab revolt. Egypt gained its independence in 1922, although it remained under British influence until 1954.

Persia
Persia (modern Iran) was an independent kingdom ruled by the shahs of the Qajar dynasty until 1925. But during the 19th century European influence increased and in 1906 a new European-style constitution was established.

Fath Ali (1797–1834, left) was the last Persian Shah to rule without European influence.

Mustafa Kemal was later known as Atatürk, meaning "father of the Turks."

Modern Turkey
After World War I (1914–18), the Allied forces occupied Istanbul and began dismantling what was left of the Ottoman state. The sultan was deposed in 1922 and Mustafa Kemal (1881–1938) set up an alternative parliament. In 1923 Turkey was declared a republic, with Kemal as its first president.

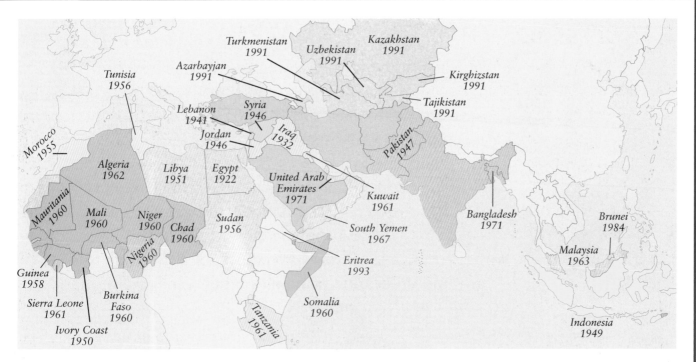

The map, with country labels and independence dates:

Turkmenistan 1991
Kazakhstan 1991
Uzbekistan 1991
Kirghizstan 1991
Azarbayjan 1991
Tunisia 1956
Lebanon 1941
Syria 1946
Tajikistan 1991
Jordan 1946
Iraq 1932
Pakistan 1947
Morocco 1955
Algeria 1962
Libya 1951
Egypt 1922
United Arab Emirates 1971
Kuwait 1961
Mauritania 1960
Mali 1960
Niger 1960
Chad 1960
Sudan 1956
South Yemen 1967
Bangladesh 1971
Brunei 1984
Malaysia 1963
Nigeria 1960
Eritrea 1993
Guinea 1958
Sierra Leone 1961
Burkina Faso 1960
Tanzania 1961
Somalia 1960
Ivory Coast 1950
Indonesia 1949

The map shows the countries of the Muslim world and the dates by which they became independent of European colonial governments or their influence.

Pakistan and Bangladesh

In 1940, when India was coming close to gaining independence, an organization called the Muslim League began to press strongly for a separate state for Indian Muslims. Pakistan was founded as two separate regions in 1947, and in 1972 the eastern region achieved its own independence as Bangladesh. Today the Muslim populations amount to 97 percent in Pakistan, 88 percent in Bangladesh, and 11 percent in India.

Decolonization

Most countries in the Muslim world gained their independence after World War II. Many of the first Muslim states were **secular** (non-religious) and had European-style constitutions and laws.

Indonesia

The Republic of Indonesia was a colony of the Netherlands from 1798 to 1945, when it was known as the Dutch East Indies. After World War II it became a republic, led by Dr. Sukarno, although it did not achieve formal independence until 1949. Today, Indonesia has by far the largest population of Muslims in the world.

Colonel Jamal Abd al-Nasir (Nassar) seized power in Egypt in 1952. British forces left two years later. Egypt's example encouraged its neighbors to expel their colonial rulers.

A return to Islam

Opposition to the formation of the Jewish state of Israel in Palestine, and other factors in the 1950s and 1960s, led to the growth of Arab nationalism. In many countries there was a return to Islamic laws and values.

Ayatollah Khomeini (left) became the leader of Iran in 1979 when the Shah was overthrown. He introduced very strict Islamic codes and ejected Western influence in dress, politics, and customs.

Women in Islam

In Muslim societies a woman's role has traditionally been seen as that of a wife and homemaker. When they get married, women have the right to receive dowries and keep their own property. They may also get divorced if a marriage is unsuccessful and causes misery. In recent times, many young women have chosen to devote more time to their educations and careers before getting married, believing that they should have more equality with young men. They have shown it is possible to stick to traditional Islamic principles while leading a modern life.

This illustration dates from around 1600. It shows an elegant woman of Isfahan, in modern Iran, writing a letter.

Women's role

In many ways Islamic traditions improved the lives of women. The Qur'an taught that all women are to be respected and protected. Men must always behave properly and decently toward them. While men are responsible for providing food and shelter for their families, women control affairs within their homes. Though this remained the custom in the Muslim world, women had an equal right to education and there were many learned women in medieval times.

Among the Rashaida people of Sudan and Ethiopia, all women wear traditional veils called burdas.

Traditional dress

The Qur'an teaches that women should always dress modestly. In many Muslim countries women have traditionally worn black, cloaklike garments, called chadors, which leave only their faces showing. Many also cover their faces with veils, called hijabs.

Outside the home

Centuries ago women were scarcely allowed outside the home in some Muslim countries, especially in cities. In 10th-century Baghdad, for example, it was felt that women should never be seen on the street. As this illustration from 16th-century Persia (left) shows, however, some women enjoyed each others' company outside the home. These women are preparing a picnic in a beautiful city garden.

Modern clothes

In recent years, many Muslim women have started to wear more modern versions of traditional, modest clothes. While they are against sex discrimination and want to have complete equality in society, they believe that many Western styles of dress are immodest or even degrading to women. Muslim women try to be graceful and feminine without being provocative or immodest.

A group of mannequins in a Cairo shop window model stylish outfits for the modern Muslim woman.

This 16th-century Persian illustration shows women sitting in a separate area of a mosque.

In the mosque

In early Islamic times women generally went to a mosque to pray. This soon became less customary, and today many women pray at home instead of in a mosque. Women with small children find this much easier. If they do want to pray at the mosque, women usually form rows behind the men or in a separate area.

Nomads

The nomadic Bedouin people of the Arabian and Sahara deserts are Muslims. They live in large tents, and the women's quarters are separated from the men's by brightly-colored woven curtains. Bedouin women (right) are highly skilled weavers of wool, using light spindles and simple looms that are easy to transport. Daughters learn the skills from their mothers at a young age.

At work

Many Muslims believe that it is right that women should be allowed to work, but they should not be forced to take jobs. Today many young Muslim women go to universities and are at least as well-educated and qualified as their brothers. They naturally want to take up professions, and in the workplace they have the right to be treated with respect.

These young Egyptian women, wearing headscarves for modesty, continue the Muslim tradition of scientific research.

The family

It was always important for a wife to produce children, especially since Muslim men were allowed to have up to four wives. If a man had all that he wanted, including a male heir, he might not take another wife. Having children, especially sons, also gave a woman a more respected position in Islamic society, and children were brought up to respect and obey their mothers.

Celebrations at the court of the Mogul emperor Akbar the Great in 1569. The joyful occasion was the birth of his first son, Salim, born to one of his numerous wives.

Benazir Bhutto became the Pakistani leader just three months after giving birth to her first child.

Politics

Toward the end of the 20th century Muslim women achieved great breakthroughs in the field of politics. In 1988 Benazir Bhutto, the daughter of the founder of her political party, became the first female leader of a Muslim country when she was elected prime minister of Pakistan. She was followed in 1991 by Khaleda Zia, who was elected prime minister of Bangladesh, and Tansu Ciller, who became Turkey's first woman leader in 1993.

Islam and the West

Increasing emigration of Muslims to Europe and the Americas during the last quarter of the 20th century was part of a worldwide movement of people who sought better jobs, education, and political and religious freedom. Muslim immigrants have formed communities and built mosques and community centers where they can meet and worship. In some cases, incomprehension has arisen among local inhabitants who do not understand or accept Muslim ways, such as **polygamy** (having more than one wife). Muslims, too, have difficulty accepting the more secular (non-religious) aspects of Western society. The goal of tolerant people everywhere is to live peacefully together, with everyone respecting beliefs and ways different from their own.

The Islamic world and Europe have always had strong trade links. This painting (right) shows ambassadors from Venice, Italy, being received at Damascus in the 15th century.

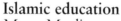

Muslims in Western Europe
Muslims emigrated to Western Europe from the 1950s onward, when European businesses were booming and extra labor was required. Many so-called "guestworkers" became accustomed to their new countries and did not return to their countries of origin when their work contracts expired.

Enriching local cultures
Muslim immigrants and communities have enriched their adopted countries with their languages, religion, food, music, and points of view. Contact between people of different cultural traditions is stimulating and leads to greater understanding and tolerance.

Islamic education
Many Muslim parents in the West are concerned about finding Islamic instruction for their children. Some are worried that in state-run schools their children will learn values that will cause them to rebel against Islam. In North America today, there are more than 1,500 Sunday schools and youth groups run by Islamic centers, while more than 100 religious schools have been licensed in various states.

Islam in North America

The Muslim community in North America is very diverse, composed of people who have arrived from many different parts of the world. The earliest immigrants came from Syria, Lebanon, Jordan, and Palestine, beginning around 1875. Changes in immigration laws during the 1960s helped the arrival of many Muslims from Bangladesh, India, and Pakistan. Of the estimated six million Muslims in the United States, the largest group is of African-Americans who were converted by the teachings of Elijah Muhammad, leader of the Nation of Islam.

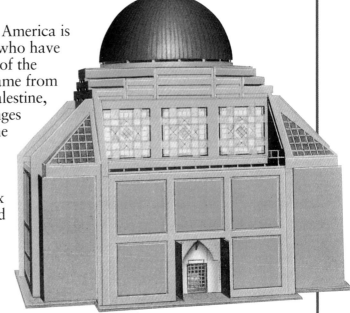

Malcolm X, disciple of Elijah Muhammad, and an important leader of the Nation of Islam until his death in 1965.

Islamic communities in the West have built an array of different types of mosques and community centers. The one shown above is the Islamic Center of New York. It is located on the Upper East Side of Manhattan.

The dramatic increase in oil prices led to an economic slowdown in the Western world.

Political and economic issues

The Middle East is one of the richest oil-producing areas in the world. Most of this oil is exported to the West. In 1973 the Muslim states in the Middle East led a move to increase oil prices, mainly to punish the U.S. for its support of Israel. The price of crude oil went from $3.00 per barrel in 1970 to $30.00 in 1980. This caused an economic downturn in the West, and a lot of bad feeling. In 1990, a multinational force led by the U.S.A. declared war on Iraq when it invaded Kuwait, to prevent the Iraqis from controlling the oil-rich state of Kuwait.

Tolerance and intolerance

In 1989 the leader of Iran, Ayatollah Khomeini, put a bounty on the head of novelist Salman Rushdie because he felt that the writer's novel *The Satanic Verses* was disrespectful toward Islam. Rushdie was forced into hiding for almost a decade until the threat was formally withdrawn in 1998. However, Islamic extremists assassinated translators and publishers associated with the book in other countries.

U.S. soldiers on the ground in Kuwait during the "Desert Storm" operation.

39

Islamic Festivals

The two most important festivals in the Islamic calendar celebrate the end of the fasting month of Ramadan and the pilgrimage to Mecca. In Islamic countries there are several days of national holidays for both festivals. Other special days throughout the year honor events in the life of Muhammad. During all these festivals Muslims take the opportunity to come together to praise Allah. They are special times when people contact others they may not have seen for a long time. Huge numbers of people gather in mosques and parks to pray and celebrate together.

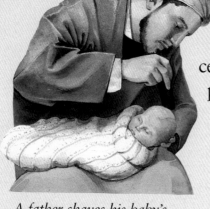

A father shaves his baby's head. According to tradition, the weight of hair – in gold or silver – is given to the poor.

Birth

The birth of a baby is a joyful event, and the child is seen as a gift from Allah. The head of the family takes the baby in his arms and whispers the words of the adhan, or call to prayer, into the child's right ear. One of the oldest relatives rubs a little honey or sugar on the baby's gums, as a symbol of sweet kindness and obedience.

The diagram shows the months of the Muslim year 1422 AH (anno Hegirae, or after the year of the Hegira), and how it relates to 2001–02 CE in the Western calendar.

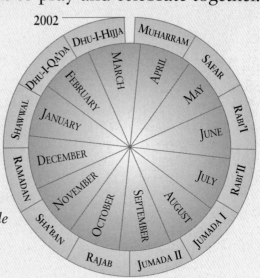

2002

MUHARRAM, SAFAR, RABI'I, II.RABI', JUMADA I, JUMADA II, RAJAB, SHA'BAN, RAMADAN, SHAWWAL, DHU-I-QA'DA, DHU-I-HIJJA

MARCH, APRIL, MAY, JUNE, JULY, AUGUST, SEPTEMBER, OCTOBER, NOVEMBER, DECEMBER, JANUARY, FEBRUARY

A Muslim bride in her special marriage costume.

The lunar calendar

The Islamic calendar is based on the lunar year – a period of twelve revolutions of the Moon around the Earth. This makes it eleven days shorter than the Western calendar and means that Islamic dates change every year in relation to Christian dates and the seasons. The first day of the first month of Muharram is celebrated by Muslims, but it is not as important as the New Year festival is to others.

Weddings

Wedding ceremonies may take place at a mosque, or at the house of either the bride or the groom. An imam is usually present, and there are prayers and readings from the Qur'an, as well as an exchange of vows in front of witnesses. A written marriage contract is usually signed before the event, and there is a celebration party after the wedding.

Muhammad's birthday

The Prophet's birthday – the festival of Mawlid al-Nabi – is celebrated on the 12th day of the third month, Rabi' al Awal. In the Western calendar, the date is traditionally August 20, 570 CE. The first large celebration of this day took place in the 13th century and quickly spread throughout the Islamic world.

Painting of the massacre at Karbala, when Husayn was killed by troops loyal to the Umayyad dynasty.

Right: Muhammad with the angel Gabriel during the night journey.

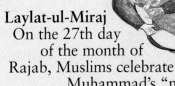

Ashura

Shi'ite Muslims remember their "Prince of martyrs," Husayn, on the tenth day of Muharram, in the festival of Ashura. Husayn was a grandson of Muhammad and son of Ali, whom Shi'ites regard as the Prophet's first true successor. In 680 Husayn and most of his supporters were massacred. Shi'ites show their grief at Ashura, with some men beating themselves with chains and others cutting themselves with swords.

Studying the Qur'an.

Laylat-ul-Barat

On the night of the full moon before the start of Ramadan – the 15th of the month of Sha'ban – many Muslims stay up and read the Qur'an. They may also visit dead relatives' graves and pray for their souls. This festival is called Laylat-ul-Barat. Muslims believe that at this time God determines everyone's fate for the coming year. It also marks the time when Muhammad began his preparations for the fast.

Breaking the fast

One of the most important Islamic festivals is Id-ul-Fitr, which begins at the sighting of the first new moon after the month of Ramadan (the new month is called Shawwal). This festival marks the breaking of the fast, and Muslims give thanks for having had the strength to complete it.

People send cards to wish others "Id Mubarak" or "Happy Id festival," and special sweet foods are prepared.

Laylat-ul-Miraj

On the 27th day of the month of Rajab, Muslims celebrate Muhammad's "night journey," when he ascended to the throne of Allah (see page 12). They gather in mosques and remember that special night, when the five daily prayers were fixed.

The Night of Power

Laylat-ul-Qadr celebrates the "Night of Power," when Muhammad received his first revelation. The festival is held during the last ten days of Ramadan, and the special night itself is on the 27th of the month. The Qur'an describes this night as "better than a thousand months."

Laylat-ul-Qadr is a time for prayer.

Sacrifice

Id-ul-Adha, the Feast of Sacrifice, takes place on the tenth day of the month of Dhu'l-Hijjah. This commemorates the sacrifice that Ibrahim was prepared to make by killing his son Ismail, and it is the same as the festival that is held on the hajj pilgrimage (see page 29). Usually a sheep or goat is sacrificed, and in many countries families have their feast animals killed at licensed slaughterhouses.

The sacrifice of a sheep or other animal represents Muslims' self-sacrifice to Allah.

Islam Today

The 20th century was a time of revival and growth for Islam. The hold of the European colonial powers gradually weakened and modern Muslim states emerged. Toward the end of the century, there was a return to Islamic laws and values in many Muslim lands. Today, there is an ongoing struggle in some Islamic countries between the more conservative religious people and those with a less traditional view of government and society.

Muslims all over the world are united by their religious beliefs. This 14th century miniature from Iraq shows the archangel Asrafil blowing the last trumpet on the day of judgement.

A return to Islam
Following the breakup of the Soviet Union in 1991 the Muslim peoples of Central Asia and the Balkans were free to worship openly again.

There were several brutal civil wars in the 1990s in the countries previously united under Soviet influence as Yugoslavia. Many Muslims from Bosnia left the area and went to live in distant Muslim countries, such as Malaysia. The Mostar bridge (left) became a symbol of the fighting between Muslims and Croats.

Muslims believe that women should always be modestly dressed. In some countries this involves wearing a headscarf, but in others it means being covered from head to foot. These women from Afghanistan are wearing a very conservative style of dress.

Mujaheddin (Muslim rebels) fought government troops to take control of Afghanistan after the Soviet withdrawal in 1988.

Islamism
During the final years of the 20th century there was growing support among Muslims for a return to stricter and more traditional interpretation of Islamic laws. The most extreme form of Islamism, or fundamentalism, has taken hold in Afghanistan where the Taliban has separated men and women, closed girls' schools, stopped women from working outside the home, banned television, movies, and music, and introduced extreme punishments for crime, such as amputation for theft.

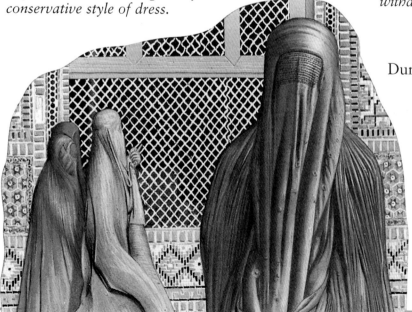

Difficult political problems, such as the question of a homeland for Palestinians, continue to plague Islamic relations with the West. Yasir Arafat (above) met many times with U.S. presidents to seek a solution.

Muslim men during prayers at a mosque in Florence, Italy.

Diversity

Diversity is perhaps the most striking thing about Islam today. Of the one billion or so Muslims in the world now, only about a quarter live in the Middle East. Indonesia has the world's largest Muslim population, and there are more Muslims in the central Asian countries that were previously part of the Soviet Union than there are in the Middle East. However, Arabic remains the language of the Qu'ran and the Middle East is the land of Islamic origin.

Into the future

As a stronger sense of Muslim identity became established in the second half of the 20th century, a number of pan-Islamic organizations were formed, such as the World Muslim League (established 1962) and the Islamic Conference (established 1969). The Islamic Conference now has more than 40 member states, including countries as far apart as Senegal and Malaysia. Despite increasing unity, conflict both among and within Muslim societies continues and the Islamic world is poised on the edge of a new century that will be dynamic and filled with challenge and change.

An imam (leader or teacher) gives his sermon from a pulpit in the mosque.

Throughout the Muslim world the mosque remains the center of the community it supports. The Great Mosque of Hassan II at Casablanca in Morocco was completed in 1993. It can hold up to 25,000 people and is part of a group of buildings that also includes a library, public baths, and an amphitheater.

GLOSSARY

Algebra: A branch of mathematics which uses logic to explain arithmetic relations. The word "algebra" itself comes from "al-jabr," which means "restoration" in Arabic. "Al-jabr" was part of the Arabic title of Muhammad al-Khwarizmi's book on mathematics.

Allah: The name of the one God in the Islamic religion.

Arabic: The language of the Arabs, the Semitic people who originated on the Arabian peninsula.

Bedouin: A nomadic Arab of the Arabian, Syrian, or North African deserts.

Black Stone: The sacred stone placed inside the Ka'bah by Ibrahim, who received it from the angel Gabriel.

Caliph: A successor of Muhammad the Prophet as a spiritual leader and head of the Muslim community.

City-state: A state which is controlled by the free citizens of an independent city, and which exerts control over those nearby territories under its power.

Dynasty: A succession of rulers from the same family's line of descent.

Five Pillars of Islam: The five duties that all Muslims must perform: profession of faith; ritual prayer; helping the needy; fasting during the month of Ramadan; and the hajj.

Hajj: A special annual pilgrimage to Mecca in the 12th month of the Islamic calendar. All Muslims must go on the hajj at least once in their lives. A man who has completed the hajj is called a hajji, and a woman is called a hajjah.

Islam: The religious faith that professes belief in Allah as the one and only God, and in Muhammad as his prophet. Followers of Islam are called Muslims.

Ka'bah: The cube-shaped shrine in the courtyard of the Great Mosque in Mecca. Muslims believe that Ibrahim built the first house for the worship of one God there. It is the most sacred spot in the world for all Muslims, who turn toward it when they pray.

Khanate: The area ruled by a khan, a local chieftan or man of rank, especially in Afghanistan, Iran, and some areas of central Asia.

Mecca: The city in modern Saudi Arabia that was the birthplace of Muhammad, and is the world's holiest city for Muslims. It is the location of the Ka'bah shrine, and the center of the Islamic pilgrimage.

Mihrab: An arched niche inside a mosque that is set into the wall opposite the entrance. When worshipers face the mihrab, they know they are facing Mecca.

Mosque: An Islamic place of public worship.

Muhammad: The Arabian prophet whom Muslims believe received revelations directly from Allah, and the founder of the Islamic religion. Also called the Prophet.

Nomad: A person who has no fixed living place, but who instead wanders from place to place in search of food and grazing land.

Polygamy: The practice of having more than one husband or wife. (In Islamic custom, it means having more than one wife.)

Qur'an: The sacred book of Islam, recognized by Muslims as containing the revelations given to Muhammad by Allah. It is the basis for the religious, social, commercial, military, and legal rules of the Islamic world.

Ramadan: The ninth month of the Islamic calendar, observed as a sacred month during which all able Muslims fast from sunrise to sunset each day.

Salah: A ritual prayer that Muslims perform five times daily, while facing Mecca.

Secular: Of or relating to things that are not spiritual or religious.

Shah: Until 1979, the absolute ruler of Iran. In 1979, after Iranian riots, the Shah left Iran, which became an Islamic republic with a Muslim leader as president.

Shari'ah: A set of commandments and laws that tell Muslims what is right, and how to lead good lives. The word literally means "path."

Simurgh: A large ancient bird from Persian legend, believed to have great wisdom.

Sufis: Muslim mystics who search for a close, personal relationship with Allah.

Sultanate: The area ruled by a sultan, a king or ruling sovereign, usually of an Islamic state.

Sunni: The largest branch of the Islamic religion, characterized by adherence to the Sunnah, or way of Muhammad, based on the Prophet's words and acts. The Sunni followers accept the first three caliphs as Muhammad's successors, and are sometimes called Orthodox Muslims.

Shi'a: One of the two main branches of Islam, characterized by non-acceptance of the first three caliphs, and the belief that the fourth caliph, Ali, was Muhammad's first true successor. Shi'a is followed by most people in Iran and Iraq.

Zakah: A form of charity or welfare collection, and the third Pillar of Islam. The word zakah literally means "cleansing."

INDEX

Acknowledgements

The Publishers would like to thank the following photographers and picture libraries for the photos used in this book.

t=top; tl=top left; tc=top center; tr=top right; c=center;
cl=center left; b=bottom; bl=bottom left; bc=bottom center; br=bottom right

Cover Marco Nardi/McRae Books Archives; **9c** Robert Azzi / Grazia Neri/W.C.A.; **25c** Corbis/Grazia Neri; **29br** Marco Nardi/McRae Books Archives; **40cl** Corbis/Grazia Neri; **41cl** Corbis/Grazia Neri; **43tr** Press Photo, Florence